IMAGES
of America

REMEMBERING HUDSON'S
THE GRANDE DAME OF DETROIT RETAILING

ON THE COVER: **FASHION DIRECTION, 1955.** Retail survives on consumer changes and demands. This main-floor ledge display is promoting forward fashions at Hudson's. (Courtesy Detroit Historical Museum.)

IMAGES
of America

REMEMBERING HUDSON'S
THE GRANDE DAME OF DETROIT RETAILING

Michael Hauser and Marianne Weldon

ARCADIA
PUBLISHING

Copyright © 2010 by Michael Hauser and Marianne Weldon
ISBN 978-0-7385-8366-2

Published by Arcadia Publishing
Charleston, South Carolina

Printed in the United States of America

Library of Congress Control Number: 2010937732

For all general information, please contact Arcadia Publishing:
Telephone 843-853-2070
Fax 843-853-0044
E-mail sales@arcadiapublishing.com
For customer service and orders:
Toll-Free 1-888-313-2665

Visit us on the Internet at www.arcadiapublishing.com

*Dedicated to the valiant individuals of the Hudson's/Target
Volunteer Retiree Association who assist and reach out to countless
nonprofit organizations throughout southeast Michigan.*

CONTENTS

ACKNOWLEDGMENTS

We gratefully acknowledge the assistance of the following individuals: Alyn Thomas of the Manning Brothers Historical Collection, Diane Edgecomb of the Central Business District Foundation, Adam Lovell and Tracy Irwin of the Detroit Historical Museum, Wanda Jazowski, Cynthia Young, and Patience Nauta. We would also like to thank our editor, Anna Wilson, for her continual faith in our projects.

INTRODUCTION

It is hard to believe today, but back in 1891 when Joseph Lowthian Hudson decided to move his successful retail operation from the former Detroit Opera House on Campus Martius to the corner of Farmer Street and Gratiot Avenue, skeptics told him he would be doomed. Many of these naysayers felt that location was too far uptown. Hudson, however, was forward thinking and had an inkling that portion of downtown would eventually become the commercial hub of southeast Michigan. His four nephews exhibited the same spirit when the downtown store was greatly expanded in future decades and again in the 1950s with Hudson's suburban expansion.

Hudson was one of Detroit's first merchants to recognize the responsibilities and opportunities of a department store as a civic leader. Until his untimely death in 1912, Hudson gave of himself and his money to a vast array of civic endeavors, ranging from the United Way to the YMCA and the Detroit Institute of Arts. Four youthful nephews stepped into the company's leadership upon Hudson's death. Richard H. Webber, Oscar Webber, James B. Webber, and Joseph L. Webber led Hudson's into its second phase of growth as a national retail leader. Each nephew exhibited a unique retailing specialization, thus forming a dynamic team. Under their stewardship, Hudson's became one of the largest retailers in the world.

Following World War I, Hudson's provided women with access to jobs that offered them independence. Store positions such as buyers, merchandise managers, and area sales managers empowered women to be on a more level playing field with men.

The family legacy continued when Joseph L. Hudson Jr. joined the firm in 1950. By 1961, at age 29, he became president of Hudson's. Joe proved to be a role model for the business community and store associates as well. He once told a gathering that Hudson's served its guests "from the cradle to the grave!"

Because of community spectaculars such as the Freedom Festival Fireworks, annual flower show, Easter show, Thanksgiving Day parade, animated windows, and elaborate holiday décor, Hudson's had a profound effect on the lives of generations of Detroiters. Folks looked upon these events as their own and integrated them into family rituals that have been passed down through generations.

Shoppers and retail workers of several generations ago supported a thriving downtown Detroit environment that included dining, sports, and entertainment. When one spoke of going downtown, they really meant Hudson's, which set the trend for consumer culture in southeast Michigan.

Hudson's was also a key vendor to many local firms, from paper and food suppliers to the media. In the 1960s, the company purchased 6.25 million lines of newspaper advertising annually, totaling 50 pages of advertising per week. One could not pick up a copy of the *Detroit Free Press* or the *Detroit News* and not find a Hudson's ad. The store kept radio and television stations busy, while printing firms, mailing houses, and the post office scrambled to distribute Hudson direct mail pieces and catalogs.

As the company branched out to the suburbs, Hudson's continued to think in a big way. Its branch locations were much larger from a square footage standpoint than other department stores around the country. Most branches averaged around 200,000 square feet, but Northland and Eastland were more than double that size. The Southland, Westland, Oakland, Genesee Valley, and Pontiac stores were around 300,000 square feet. Later branch stores, including Fairlane, Twelve Oaks, and Lakeside, were around 200,000 square feet. Of course, this was a time when the department store was all things to all people and before the advent of specialty and big-box retailers. By the end of the 1990s, Hudson's was firmly ensconced in Michigan with stores in Ann Arbor, Battle Creek, Grand Rapids, Kalamazoo, Lansing, Port Huron, Saginaw, and Traverse City.

Today's consumers only know department stores as being anchors for regional shopping centers. Other than being part of a mall promotion, there is little community involvement on the scale once enjoyed when Hudson's was a hometown hero. Perhaps this is why young people today have such a yearning for information about what locals once had, not only with Hudson's, but when downtown Detroit had become one of the most vibrant retail centers in North America. Hopefully they will find a way to bring back some of the excitement that was once shared by so many generations before and can then pass that on to their families.

One

THE BUILDING

THE BIG STORE EMERGES ON WOODWARD AVENUE, 1919. In this view of the Gratiot Avenue end of the Woodward frontage, Hudson's has not yet acquired the buildings housing Himelhoch's Women's Apparel in the center and National Silks on the southern end of the block. The banner is encouraging the public to purchase post–World War I war bonds. (Courtesy Manning Brothers Historical Collection.)

WOODWARD AVENUE EXPANSION, 1914. The William A. Albrecht Company is erecting steel for the 10-story Woodward addition to Hudson's in this image. The original 1891 "Big Red Store" building on Farmer Street sits behind the Woodward frontage. Smith, Hinchman and Grylls were the architects for all of the store additions. (Courtesy Detroit Historical Museum.)

LOOKING SOUTH ON WOODWARD AVENUE, 1918. Yet another Woodward parcel is secured for the Hudson store. The Ferry Building on the left housed a portion of the Newcomb Endicott and Company department store. Newcomb's was a formidable competitor until Hudson's acquired it in 1927. (Courtesy Manning Brothers Historical Collection.)

WOODWARD AVENUE, LOOKING NORTH FROM GRATIOT AVENUE, 1921. By now, Hudson's had prominent frontage on Woodward, with the exception of several holdouts such as Sallan Jewelers, Himelhoch's, and Newcomb's at the Grand River Avenue end of the block. Building signage features the distinctive JLH logo. (Courtesy Central Business District Foundation.)

HUDSON'S ACQUIRES HIMELHOCH'S BUILDING, 1923. At last, Hudson's was able to acquire the Himelhoch's store, demolish the building, and construct a 10-story addition to join the other portions of its Woodward Avenue buildings. There is a consistency in the architecture in the various additions. Two of Newcomb Endicott's buildings are on the north end of the block at Grand River Avenue. (Courtesy Manning Brothers Historical Collection.)

HUDSON'S MUSIC STORE ANNEX, 1923. Hudson's leased this structure, the former home of Jerome Remick Music Publishing on Liberty Street, from 1914 to 1931. Located here were pianos, organs, radios, victrolas, sheet music, and recorded music. The store moved to the 13th floor of the Woodward Avenue building in 1931. (Courtesy Manning Brothers Historical Collection.)

FARMER STREET BUILDING REPLACEMENT NEARS COMPLETION, 1925. Construction workers feverishly work to complete the 15-story Farmer addition to Hudson's. This structure replaced the original 1891 "Big Red Store" that originally stood on this block. During construction, various departments were consolidated into the Woodward Avenue building. (Courtesy Manning Brothers Historical Collection.)

DEMOLISHING NEWCOMB ENDICOTT AND COMPANY STORE, 1927. Following the purchase of Newcomb's, Hudson's began to demolish those buildings for a major expansion at the Grand River Avenue end of the block. This expansion was heralded as "The Greater Hudson Store," because as the sign on the right declares, "The progress of Detroit demands it." (Courtesy Manning Brothers Historical Collection.)

FARMER STREET AND GRAND RIVER AVENUE PRIOR TO DEMOLITION, 1927. This view through overhead streetcar wires is after Hudson's purchased the Newcomb Endicott Company. Newcomb's had frontage on Farmer Street and Grand River Avenue and a 12-story tower on Woodward Avenue, as well as the four-story Ferry Building on Woodward. (Courtesy Detroit Historical Museum.)

STRUCTURAL STEEL RISES FOR HUDSON'S NORTH ADDITION, 1928. Here a dramatic image captures the L-shaped addition being constructed on the site of the former Newcomb Endicott store. To the left, the 1923 Farmer Street building can be viewed, and to the right are the various Woodward Avenue additions. (Courtesy Manning Brothers Historical Collection.)

THE MIGHTY HUDSON TOWER NEARING COMPLETION, 1928. As viewed from Farmer Street, the massiveness of the Hudson store nearing completion is evident. This addition includes the 25-story tower and the 15-story addition on the Grand River Avenue end. Before the Grand River addition was even completed, the decision was made to add two floors to that end of the structure. (Courtesy Manning Brothers Historical Collection.)

FARMER STREET EXTERIOR, 1928. This image was taken prior to the construction of the new downtown branch of the Detroit Public Library. Kern's department store is on the far left. In the foreground, some young children are enjoying a rare patch of green in the middle of downtown. (Courtesy Detroit Historical Museum.)

FARMER STREET AT GRAND RIVER AVENUE, 1949. Hudson's was still changing all of its window displays on Woodward, Grand River, and Gratiot Avenues and on Farmer Street on a weekly basis. Sallan Jewelers is at a new location in the far right corner on the west side of Woodward Avenue. Sallan was displaced when the 1946 Woodward addition to Hudson's was completed. (Courtesy Manning Brothers Historical Collection.)

WOODWARD AVENUE AT GRAND RIVER AVENUE, 1928. This view shows the 1928 addition on the left and 1910–1911 structures on the right. This year also saw four large illuminated signs erected emblazoning the name "HUDSON'S" on all four sides of the tower. Each sign was 60 feet long and required a framework of steel weighing almost 4 tons. (Courtesy Manning Brothers Historical Collection.)

BUSTLING WOODWARD AVENUE FRONTAGE, 1959. The 1950s proved to be very good years for downtown Hudson's. Even though Northland and Eastland were well established by this time, the downtown store still racked up impressive sales figures. The famous Kern's clock is on the right at the Ernst Kern Company department store. (Courtesy Manning Brothers Historical Collection.)

Two

THE WAR YEARS

HUDSON'S SALES OF WAR BONDS, 1942. War bonds were debt securities issued by the U.S. government to finance military operations, stabilize prices, and prevent inflation during World War II. Hudson's was the first American department store appointed by the U.S. Treasury to be an issuing agent for war bond purchases. Between May 1, 1942 and April 14, 1943, more than $5 million in bonds were sold at Hudson's. (Courtesy Detroit Historical Museum.)

VICTORY LOAN DRIVE AT HUDSON'S, 1943. To match the 1,290 Hudson employees in the service, each of the 1,290 brigadier gallants (store associates actively selling war bonds) sponsored one of those servicemen to "Back the Attack" for them personally. At the close of the drive, each brigadier sent a personal victory mail message with autographs of bond customers to those soldiers. (Courtesy Detroit Historical Museum.)

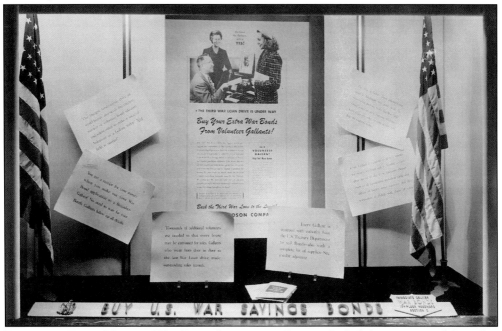

PROMOTING EXTRA HOLIDAY WAR BOND SALES, 1943. During the holiday season, each brigadier gallant suggested to the undecided guest to purchase a Christmas gift bond folder. Hudson's was awarded the Minuteman flag by the U.S. Treasury in 1943, proclaiming that 90 percent of store employees were allotting a portion of their salaries to war savings bonds. (Courtesy Detroit Historical Museum.)

HUDSON'S WINDOWS DEVOTED TO PATRIOTIC EFFORTS, 1942. Besides devoting Woodward Avenue windows to the war effort, Hudson's set up 30 stations throughout the store for the sale of war bonds. Additionally, Hudson employees sold victory corsages and boutonnieres, which consisted of nine 10¢ war stamps selling for $1. Further support included full-page newspaper ads and radio spots. (Courtesy Detroit Historical Museum.)

THE QUIZ KIDS INVADE DETROIT, 1943. *Quiz Kids* was a popular radio series sponsored by Alka-Seltzer. The program asked questions sent in by listeners, with the answers supplied by a panel of five children who were selected for their high IQs. Hudson's brought *Quiz Kids* to the Masonic Temple as part of the Four Freedoms War Bond Show. (Courtesy Detroit Historical Museum.)

PROMOTING MICHIGAN PREMIERE OF *STAGE DOOR CANTEEN*, 1943. Hudson's devoted a window to promote this film, debuting at downtown's Palms State Theatre. The movie celebrated the importance of New York's Stage Door Canteen, which served as a recreational center for American servicemen on leave. The canteen regularly featured stars of Broadway, film, and big bands. (Courtesy Detroit Historical Museum.)

FORGING AHEAD WITH THE THIRD WAR LOAN EFFORT, 1943. Hudson's also set up a special war bond issuing booth at a submarine exhibit in Grand Circus Park and sold $20,000 in bonds the first day. The Third War Loan effort ended with the Four Freedoms War Bond Show, sponsored by Hudson's, the Treasury Department, and *The Saturday Evening Post*. (Courtesy Detroit Historical Museum.)

PROMOTING VICTORY MAIL, 1944. This Woodward Avenue window featured one of the world's most popular pinup models, Ginger Rogers, promoting V-mail. Victory mail operated during World War II to expedite mail service for American armed forces overseas. (Courtesy Detroit Historical Museum.)

U.S. NAVY VICTORY MAIL EXHIBIT AT HUDSON'S, 1945. An interesting exhibit in the 12th-floor auditorium included demonstrations by U.S. Navy men and WAVES (Women Accepted for Volunteer Emergency Service) on how to operate the machines that sped victory mail on its way overseas. The exhibit also included trophies and souvenirs from the battlefronts of the world. (Courtesy Detroit Historical Museum.)

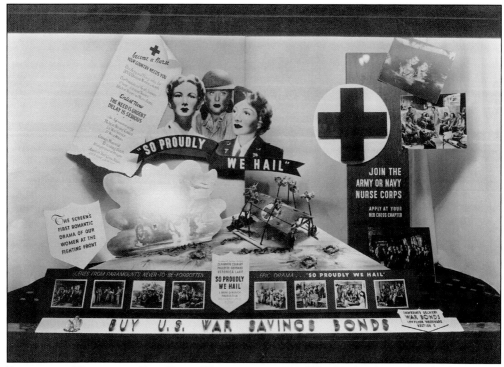

RECRUITING NURSES AND RED CROSS VOLUNTEERS, 1943. This Hudson's window display sought volunteers for the war effort by teaming up with a promotion for the film *So Proudly We Hail*, a love story featuring American women on the fighting front. This was an opportunity for those without family obligations to thank their country by volunteering with the Army or Navy Nurse Corps. (Courtesy Detroit Historical Museum.)

DISPLAY DEVOTED TO U.S. MARINE CORPS WOMEN'S RESERVE, 1945. This reserve branch of the Marine Corps was established in 1942 to provide women for shore duty jobs so men could be released for combat duty. Requirements stated that these women had to be 20 to 36 years of age and high school graduates. (Courtesy Detroit Historical Museum.)

IN-HOUSE MAGAZINE PROMOTES WAR BONDS, 1942. *Hudsonian*, the in-house magazine produced by Hudson's, began in 1923 and with the exception of the Depression years was published continuously through the early 1980s. The issue shown here with a young child licking a war bond stamp is encouraging employees to save every penny to support the war effort. (Courtesy Michael Hauser.)

HUDSON'S VOLUNTEER BRIGADIER GALLANTS, 1943. Another issue of *Hudsonian* was dedicated to those employees who pledged to sell at least $1,000 worth of war bonds in the Third Victory Loan. Brigadier Gallants was an organization of loyal, patriotic Hudson's employees out to break all records in the sale of war bonds. (Courtesy Michael Hauser.)

Seventh War Loan Drive on Woodward Avenue, 1945. To rally support for war bond sales, Hudson's erected a massive seven-story banner on the Woodward side of the store along with smaller banners above the marquee. Loudspeakers were also set up to capture shoppers' attention. (Courtesy Michael Hauser.)

Three

CHILDREN AND
THE HOLIDAYS!

MARIONETTE THEATER, C. 1930. For many years, the holidays would not be complete without marionettes that could dance, walk, or swing out on command. Hudson's annually featured marionette shows and the wildly popular Victor Puppet Opera Troupe, which featured 205 puppets that sang and danced the popular operas of the day. (Courtesy Detroit Historical Museum.)

PRECISION HAIRCUTS WHILE RIDING A BULL MOOSE, 1928. Hudson's famous Circus Land Barber Shop on the fourth floor of the Farmer Street building was designed by Tony Sarg, a well-known artist of the time. Sarg also created the marionettes that were featured in the barbershop. (Courtesy Detroit Historical Museum.)

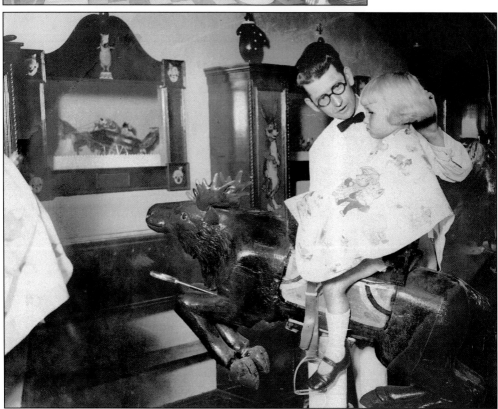

BACK WHEN A HAIRCUT AT HUDSON'S WAS A HOLIDAY, 1928. The Circus Land Barber Shop was heralded as the only barbershop of its kind in the world when it opened. Fifteen wild animal chairs kept children, as well as adults, amused and happy. The adjacent waiting room also featured marionette shows. (Courtesy Detroit Historical Museum.)

The CHILDREN'S MAGAZINE

from THE J. L. HUDSON COMPANY

Vol. 5, No. 6	DETROIT, MICHIGAN	June, 1929

How Many of These Flowers Do You Know?

A Garden Tragedy

There was a chubby little Gnome who lived in a flower garden alone.

He would pull up new plants just to see what made them grow and tear the buds off the flower stems.

This day he began by throwing Snowballs at Bachelor Button, who was very cross.

Sweet William said to him, "Some day Tiger Flower or maybe Dandelion will eat you for being so naughty."

But the little Gnome didn't believe that and continued in his wicked ways.

He saw a Bleeding Heart and tore it up just to see if it really would bleed.

That made pretty Brown-eyed Susan cry and Snapdragon became very angry and snapped the little Gnome up and swallowed him.

Brown-eyed Susan told Sweet William where he was and he reached right into the Snapdragon's mouth and pulled the Gnome out, then he took a Lady's Slipper and spanked him well.

And the little Gnome was never cruel to the Flowers again.

The Three Wise Men

Three wise men of Gotham,
Went to sea in a bowl.
If the bowl had been stronger
My story would have been longer.

This picture of The Three Wise Men will be sent to all the children submitting colored pictures of Lois Marie and her baby sister Rosalee. You will find them on the next page. The picture of the Three Wise Men sent to you will be very much enlarged. It will be nice to paste in your scrapbook or hung in your playhouse.

> Will all the boys and girls who are twins send me snapshots of themselves for our snapshot page.

3

We Have Received Good Stories and Poems from These Children

Barbara Neilsen, Georgia Cocas, Jenny Tasciszewska, Betsy Armstrong, Nance Koch, Martha Miller, Marguerite Smith, Betty Crawford, Jane Cartwright, Anna Ficay, Rose Barbane, Jane Smith, Julia Baker, Harriet Goodman, Blanche Demure, Zilpha Shaver, Marion Klotz, Seymon Edell, Edward Duck, Mary Eileen Dottener, Ruth Munson, Isabelle Ducharme, Helen Apfel, Paul Gilleo, Dorothy Parker, Phyllis Bennett, V. Zahlonte, Mary Wolska, Helen McCabe, Marie LaVasco, Mildred Neubauer, Vervonia Vodraska, Edith Ann Evans, Marion Bader, and Gretchen Ann Schoenfeld.

These Children Won the Picture Contest

Gerald Harrington, age 4, of 16158 Tuller Ave., won the book, Pinocchio In America, by Angelo Patri.

And Rosalee Schwartz, age 9, of 3236 Webb Ave., won the book, Water Babies, by Kingsley.

Veronica Chambers, age 13, of 2752 Montgomery Ave., won the Complete Beginners' Stamp Collectors' Outfit.

HUDSON'S OWN CHILDREN'S MAGAZINE, 1929. This complimentary magazine, produced by Hudson's, was distributed to 50,000 guests each month; the publication accepted no advertising. Each issue featured a whimsical picture that invited children to color and send in for a prize. Winning pictures were then displayed in the fourth-floor exhibition area. The magazine also included short stories and snapshots submitted by youngsters. (Courtesy Michael Hauser.)

MEZZANINE SODA FOUNTAIN, 1928. One of the most popular stops at Hudson's for children and adults alike was located in the Farmer Street building. Menu favorites included peach shortcake, maple marshmallow walnut layer cake, peppermint frosted marble layer cake, and frozen strawberry sundaes and floats. (Courtesy Detroit Historical Museum.)

CHILDREN'S SHOE DEPARTMENT, 1949. Children's merchandise was located on the fourth floor, where all departments were arranged according to the progressive ages of children—from pinning blanket to age 16. There was even a special candy shop on this floor. (Courtesy Detroit Historical Museum.)

Hi-Yo, Silver, Away! Live From Detroit, 1938. Besides showcasing an entire block of Woodward Avenue windows, Hudson's set up a special trading post on the fourth floor where fans could get their photographs taken and purchase specially created Lone Ranger merchandise that included lunch boxes, board games, and cap guns. (Courtesy Detroit Historical Museum.)

Promoting Children's Favorites, 1946. This Hudson's window display features books that appealed to children. Favorites included Mother Goose, Humpty Dumpty, Hans Brinker, and other known figures associated with nursery rhymes and fairy tales. Each May, the store sponsored a weeklong children's book festival. (Courtesy Detroit Historical Museum.)

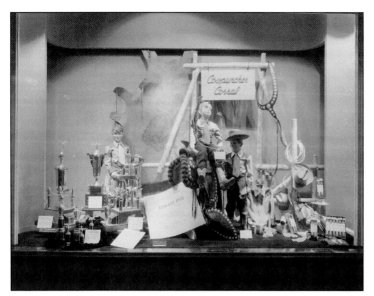

ROPING IN CHILDREN'S CLOTHING BUSINESS, 1948. This Hudson's window capitalizes on the cowboy craze of the day. Tie-ins included a Wild West theater and pony rides. Another way that Hudson's cultivated children's business was by sponsoring a concert series at Music Hall featuring the Detroit Symphony Orchestra. (Courtesy Detroit Historical Museum.)

HEADING BACK TO SCHOOL, C. 1950. By the time that children's departments became traffic generators in the mid-1920s, Hudson's elected to devote an entire floor to boys' and girls' clothing. Store management viewed the move as a good way to attract mothers and offered incentives such as clubs, contests, and special events. (Courtesy Detroit Historical Museum.)

ANTICIPATION MOUNTS FOR GOODFELLOWS SHOPPING DAY, 1956. These happy youngsters in the children's shoe department are participating in the annual Old Newsboys Goodfellows Fund special shopping day. The sole mission of the organization was to ensure that there is "no kiddie without a Christmas." The charity distributed gifts to children throughout Detroit. (Courtesy Central Business District Foundation.)

HOLIDAY REGALIA ON HUDSON'S MAIN FLOOR, 1947. Detroiters made a pilgrimage to Hudson's each holiday season to be dazzled by the décor, and they were never disappointed, including in 1982—the final holidays for the downtown store. That year, traditions around the world was the theme, which included an exhibit of 150 Currier and Ives hand-colored lithographs. (Courtesy Detroit Historical Museum.)

NOT QUITE A TEENAGER YET, 1953. The subteen shop on the fourth floor catered to young girls just shy of becoming full-fledged teenagers. This group of guests craved the same special attention and treatment accorded to teens and adults. Hudson's reached this age group via magazines, clubs, and a Fashionette advisory board. (Courtesy Detroit Historical Museum.)

NORMAN ROCKWELL HOLIDAY CARDS FROM HALLMARK, 1949. The combination of Norman Rockwell's artistic talents with Hallmark's marketing skills led to the popular success of a line of greeting cards. There were 21 paintings adapted for holiday cards, as seen in this Hudson's window. (Courtesy Detroit Historical Museum.)

SPECIAL GIFTS FOR SPECIAL FOLKS, 1947. Hudson's commercial gift service allowed business customers to select distinguished gifts in multiple price categories. The store could even send a representative to a client's office. Unlike with today's gift cards, refunds were offered for gifts not redeemed within four months. (Courtesy Michael Hauser.)

TRIM A TREE, 1954. This 10th-floor department was well stocked with garlands, glass ornaments, simulated evergreens, nativity sets, spray-on snow, ribbons, and gift wrap. Domestic and imported glass ornaments were the best-selling items. (Courtesy Detroit Historical Museum.)

THE STAG LINE STARTS HERE, 1956. From the 1950s through the 1970s, one of Hudson's holiday specialty areas was the For Men Only shop. This was a haven for males to shop for their significant others that featured hostesses to assist with gift selections. Typically this temporary area served up to 5,000 guests. (Courtesy Detroit Historical Museum.)

PEACE ON EARTH WINDOW, 1957. The decade of the 1950s saw retailers deal with critics who felt department stores were commercializing the holidays with too many representations of Santa, toys, and parades. Hudson's solution was to devote a large window for the display of a nativity scene. The store also scheduled more public appearances of the Hudson Carolers, an in-house choral group. (Courtesy Detroit Historical Museum.)

MAIN FLOOR AISLES OF BEAUTY LEDGES, 1959. The "It's Christmastime at Hudson's" slogan began in 1926, providing a keynote for the entire store. Months of planning and scheduling each year resulted in a consistent visual look throughout the store in displays, show windows, gift catalogs, on holiday gift wrap, and marketing efforts. (Courtesy Detroit Historical Museum.)

ACRES AND ACRES OF TOYS, 1941. Each holiday season, Hudson's Toytown became a land of enchantment for the entire family. With 40 percent of the year's business conducted in November and December, Toytown literally doubled in size to satisfy customer demand. At its peak, Toytown employed 180 sales associates. (Courtesy Detroit Historical Museum.)

PARADE OF TOYS, 1946. Each holiday season, Toytown would feature a different theme. This image depicts the "Adventures of Betty and Bubb." Another annual Toytown visit for many years was the Kimport doll exhibit. This display included hundreds of different dolls from around the globe. (Courtesy Detroit Historical Museum.)

HOLIDAY WINDOW AMAZEMENT, C. 1960. Children adored all of the holiday-related activities that Hudson's annually staged. Parents and grandparents also approved, as they were able to incorporate events such as Santa, auditorium spectacles, parades, Toyland, and magic shows into memorable family traditions. (Courtesy Central Business District Foundation.)

THE HUDSONIAN

It's Christmas Time at Hudson's
1940

HUDSONIAN COVER WITH KRIS KRINGLE, 1940. This issue of Hudson's in-house magazine included stories on its Thanksgiving Day parade, the Hudson Carolers, employee news and promotions, and a story on the Hudson hockey team, known as the Green Hornets, who were champions of the Metropolitan Hockey League for several years. (Courtesy Michael Hauser.)

THE HUDSONIAN
CHRISTMAS
1942

THE WAR OVERSHADOWS CONTENT IN HUDSONIAN, 1942. Another issue of *Hudsonian* covered various aspects of World War II. The smiling child on the cover has war bonds in her stocking. Stories inside highlighted parade floats that were donated to the war effort, gasoline rationing, and stories on the 575 Hudson employees then serving in World War II. (Courtesy Michael Hauser.)

SANTA AND WIMPY, 1942. These keepsake booklets were distributed each holiday season to children who visited Santaland on the 12th floor. By the 1940s, these booklets were being created by two talented Hudson employees—Jean Sharley, a fashion writer, and Mary Hale, a children's artist in the advertising department. (Courtesy Michael Hauser.)

SANTA AND SUSIE, 1944. Typically these delightful holiday booklets consisted of 16 pages, containing 20 or more illustrations. Over 100,000 copies were distributed each holiday season. Today these are collector's items and can frequently be found at ephemera shows and on eBay. (Courtesy Michael Hauser.)

SANTA'S MAGIC CASTLE ON HUDSON'S MARQUEE, 1964. Part of the delight of Hudson's Thanksgiving Day parade was the excellent craftsmanship of the floats. It took the combined efforts of many store employees to make the parade a success, including carpenters, floor service, delivery, and warehouse associates. (Courtesy Central Business District Foundation.)

CROWD IN FRONT OF HUDSON'S, 1963. This image captures the excitement of Santa's arrival atop the marquee at Hudson's. Detroit received the official greeting here from Santa, proclaiming that the holiday season had officially began. The crowds in front of Hudson's were so thick a person could not even see the pavement. (Courtesy Central Business District Foundation.)

COME TO
hudson's
SANTA PARADE

THANKSGIVING
DAY
9:30 A.M.

WOODWARD AVE.
FROM PUTNAM
TO HUDSON'S

You're all invited to our
52nd march down
Woodward Ave. in cele-
bration of the day Santa
proclaims Detroit his
'home for the holidays'.
Join us for the pure fun
and frivolity that only the
Hudson's Santa Parade
provides.

MAGAZINE AD PROMOTING SANTA PARADE, 1976. The parade route changed in 1956, marching down Woodward Avenue from Putnam Street to Hudson's. This was now possible due to the elimination of DSR (Department of Street Railways) streetcar service on Woodward Avenue and repaving of the street. Prior to 1956, the parade formed at Second Boulevard and Amsterdam Street and proceeded south on Second to Vernor Highway and then east on Vernor to Woodward. (Courtesy Michael Hauser.)

You'll agree, there **is** a
Santa Claus when you
visit **Hudson's Giftarama**

For you career girls, this is a perfect Christmas shopping spot. You'll find imagina-
tive, fun-type gifts under $10 for every feminine name on your list. Gifts that cater
to hobbies, whims, personalities. Counter after counter of displays, rich in ideas.
And, in addition, there are lots of stocking-stuffer type gifts for everybody on your
list, and they're just $1 to $3. So easy to shop in Giftarama—just take an express
elevator to the 7th Floor, Downtown, and there you are—in Christmasland.
You will find Giftaramas in Hudson's
Northland and Eastland stores, too. **HUDSON'S**

GIFTS ON THE GO, 1962. Trying not to be sexist, Hudson's opened up Giftarama shops in the
early 1960s that featured gifts exclusively for women. In the downtown store, customers could
even take an express elevator to the seventh floor where this special department was located.
(Courtesy Michael Hauser.)

Four

Unique Services and Special Events

Hudson's Book Department, 1937. This popular destination on the mezzanine hosted an annual book fair that drew thousands to the store. In 1952, the entire department was renovated and arranged by classification, making selection easier, and even included a new special-order desk. (Courtesy Detroit Historical Museum.)

AN ANNUAL RITE OF SPRING, 1945. Hudson's annual spring flower and garden show began in 1936. Elaborate live displays from around the world graced the Woodward Avenue windows, the main floor, and the 12th-floor auditorium. The 1959 show featured 5,000 plants, 100,000 blooms, and 500 different species. (Courtesy Detroit Historical Museum.)

FRESH FLOWERS, 1955. Hudson's flower market, a late addition to the downtown store, was located on the fourth floor. This department was a member of Florists' Telegraph Delivery (FTD), now Florists' Transworld Delivery, and was able to wire guest orders anywhere out of town. The company delivered locally to homes, hospitals, weddings, and funeral homes. (Courtesy Detroit Historical Museum.)

BRIDAL SERVICES FROM START TO FINISH, 1953. Hudson's bridal service began in 1937, with the store providing assistance to 3,000 brides that year. By 1970, the number grew to 17,000 brides a year. For many years, Hudson's bridal associates would even attend to the bride and groom at their home, hotel, or church. (Courtesy Detroit Historical Museum.)

WEDDING CONSULTANT EXTRAORDINAIRE, 1953. This display touts the various services offered by Carolyn Chase, Hudson's wedding consultant. Chase provided detailed information about procedure, etiquette, and wedding arrangements. She then directed the bride to service representatives for clothing selection and accessories. (Courtesy Detroit Historical Museum.)

PETS FOR ALL TYPES OF FOLKS, 1937. The pet shop was originally housed on the 10th floor, later moving to more convenient quarters on the second floor. This image notes that Hudson's is sponsoring an appearance of the Siamese cats featured in the film *The Good Earth*, which had its Detroit premiere at the Cass Theatre. (Courtesy Detroit Historical Museum.)

MOUTHWATERING CANDIES, 1935. The candy department at Hudson's was frequently modified during the war years due to sugar and chocolate shortages. Besides prime space on the main floor, there was a candy outpost on the fourth floor, and in 1951 the store opened a candy kitchen in the new Shoppers Parking Garage on Broadway Street. (Courtesy Detroit Historical Museum.)

SAY CHEESE, PRETTY PLEASE, 1938. The O'Connor Studios were located on the mezzanine for the upstairs store and in the second basement for budget store guests. Besides offering photograph services, this studio also handled wedding portraits and remounted and repaired historical images. (Courtesy Detroit Historical Museum.)

ANYONE FOR A COLD WAVE? 1948. In 1947, with the renovation of the seventh floor for the Woodward Shops, the beauty salon was forced to move to spacious new quarters on the 14th floor of the Woodward Avenue building. Salon Americana was the largest salon in town and even offered express elevator service for those who were in a hurry for a new "do." (Courtesy Detroit Historical Museum.)

CUSTOM FRAMING DEPARTMENT, 1948. This department at Hudson's complemented the Studio of Interior Design and the home furnishings model rooms. Here customers could have photographs, prints, or paintings framed. The store offered a plethora of colors and styles for both frames and mattes. (Courtesy Detroit Historical Museum.)

EXERCISE EQUIPMENT, C. 1930. Hudson's was a retailer for the Battle Creek Equipment Company line of health appliances. This department was located on the mezzanine and featured infrared lamps, steam bath cabinets, rowing machines, stationary exercise bicycles, massage belts, and treadmills. (Courtesy Detroit Historical Museum.)

PERSONALIZED BED LINENS, C. 1930. Monograms were once considered great holiday gifts on bed sheets and pillowcases. Utica introduced needlecrest monograms for its products in 1934. Demand was great enough that Hudson's staffed the monogramming outpost on the third floor with three sales associates. (Courtesy Detroit Historical Museum.)

MAP CENTER ON THE MEZZANINE, 1943. Long before the Internet or GPS systems, folks would come to Hudson's to purchase maps, globes, and atlases for assistance with their travels. This was also a popular stop for students and educators. (Courtesy Detroit Historical Museum.)

FROM TIGER ACTION

TO SUMMER THEATRE

Nye in "Charlie's Aunt".

Whether your favorite pastime is rooting for the Detroit Tigers or applauding the latest dramatic show—Hudson's has the tickets you want. From first-run movies, including Cinerama, to first-rate lectures . . . from Masonic Temple events to Olympia Stadium specials . . . we've tickets for every taste, every type of entertainment.

Have a special yen for summer theatre? Get tickets for the upcoming Northland Summer Playhouse series, including favorites like Louie

Best news of all, you can use your Hudson Charge Account for all your tickets . . . even order by phone if you choose. Just call CA 3-5100. Or visit Hudson's Ticket Service, Downtown, 4th, adjacent to the Customers' Lounge; also available, Cashier's Offices at Northland, Eastland, and Westland.

HUDSON'S

IN THE DAYS BEFORE TICKETMASTER, 1960. This ad is touting the fact that shoppers could purchase tickets not only for sporting events and concerts but for first-run films and lectures. Customers could use Hudson's charge accounts to purchase tickets either in person or over the phone—and best of all, no handling fees! (Courtesy Michael Hauser.)

Touting the Unique Attributes of Hudson's, 1961. An ad placed in magazines in the 1960s reinforced the fact that Detroit's hometown store was indeed world-renowned. When people spoke of going downtown, they really meant Hudson's, because both were so interrelated. In the days before big-box retailing, this was the place to visit to accomplish multiple tasks. (Courtesy Michael Hauser.)

HUDSON'S D·D·D SAVINGS Celebration

Monday, Tuesday and Wednesday, May 17, 18 and 19, Hudson's joins in celebrating Downtown Detroit Days. Find scores of exciting values on almost every floor of the Downtown store. Mystery Shoppers will award hundreds of gifts in the Downtown area.

Win important prizes during the DDD event

Over $6,000 worth of gifts will be awarded at one big drawing, Thursday, May 20, on the "Living Show", WWJ-Channel 4, between 9 and 10 A.M. Prizes include: 1965 Plymouth Sport Fury Convertible, RCA Color Television Set, Two 1-Week All Expense Paid Family Vacations on Boatel Houseboat, Deluxe Car-Tel Tent, Lady Gibson Electric Range, Hamilton Deluxe Gas Dryer, others. Just fill out an entry blank, deposit it in one of the boxes on Hudson's First Floor or at DSR Terminal in Capitol Park, by 9 P.M., Wednesday, May 19.

HUDSON'S

DOWNTOWN DETROIT DAYS, 1965. This biannual event was staged each May and October. Hudson's buyers would make special purchases as well as feature merchandise that only went on sale during this shopping festival. The downtown store would rack up million-dollar sales days during the annual DDDays. (Courtesy Michael Hauser.)

**hudson's...
a world
within a store**

Friends, delegates, conventioneers...welcome to our world. Where you'll find the best our city has to offer...in a festive atmosphere we've put on just for you. See our American Art Exhibit & Sale. Our fabulous display of First Ladies' gowns. Our shop devoted exclusively to 1980 GOP commemoratives. And for shopping, snacking, dining and those little necessities you forgot to pack...Hudson's is the only name you need remember. Discover our world, while you're here. We're right next door, all over town. See the Detroit area map in the center supplement of this publication for store locations.

American Art Exhibit & Sale: Wednesday through Sunday, July 9-13, at Briarwood and Oakland. Monday through Saturday, July 14-19, Downtown and Twelve Oaks.

First Ladies' Gown Exhibit: Sunday, July 6 through Sunday, July 20 at Downtown only.

There's a Hudson's store near you: DOWNTOWN/Detroit: Woodward-Grand River • NORTHLAND/Southfield: 8 Mile-Northwestern • EASTLAND/Harper Woods: 8 Mile-Kelly • WESTLAND/Westland: Warren-Wayne Roads • OAKLAND/Troy: I-75 and 14 Mile • SOUTHLAND/Taylor: Eureka between I-75-Telegraph • FAIRLANE/Dearborn: Southfield-Michigan Ave. • TWELVE OAKS/Novi: I-96 at Novi Road • LAKESIDE/Sterling Heights: Hall, east of Van Dyke • BRIARWOOD/Ann Arbor: I-94 and State Street • GENESEE VALLY/Flint: Miller Road, off I-75

100TH ANNIVERSARY AD, 1981. "A world within a store" was the overall theme for Hudson's 100th anniversary. This slogan was featured in radio, television, and print ads as well as on signage and shopping bags. There was also a special exhibit at the Detroit Historical Museum commemorating the occasion and an anniversary video. (Courtesy Michael Hauser.)

SPECTACULAR AUDITORIUM EVENTS, 1953. The 12th-floor auditorium staged everything from flower shows, auto shows, and camping exhibits to the famous Santaland walk-through. Other events included telephone shows, fragrance events, back-to-school events and even cat and dog shows. This in-store auditorium was truly the civic center of its day. (Courtesy Detroit Historical Museum.)

DETROIT: THE CITY OF TOMORROW, 1956. This exhibit in the auditorium was created and assembled as a public service by Hudson's and cosponsored by the Detroit Tomorrow Committee and Detroit's City Planning Division. Highlights focused on current and future challenges the city faced using scale models and architectural renderings. (Courtesy Detroit Historical Museum.)

Basement Store Women's Accessories, 1950. George Preston guided the Basement Store from less than 20 departments in 1915 to its position as the world's largest downstairs store featuring 600 sales associates and eight million transactions a year. The Basement Store staged fashion shows each week at clubs, high schools, and church meetings. (Courtesy Detroit Historical Museum.)

Basement Store Men's Department, 1940. The Basement Store initially concentrated on ready-to-wear fashions and later added home goods. This store-within-a-store was accessible via two escalators, four direct street entrances, nine inside stairways, and two elevators. All merchandise sold in Hudson's Basement Store was purchased especially for selling in that section. (Courtesy Detroit Historical Museum.)

MICHIGAN ON CANVAS, 1948. In 1946, Hudson's commissioned a series of 100 paintings and drawings interpreting and permanently recording contemporary life in Michigan. Executed by 10 of the country's leading artists, the paintings covered industry, farming, lake shipping, education, wildlife, and recreation. (Courtesy Detroit Historical Museum.)

TRANSPORTING THOSE PAINTINGS, 1948. Hudson's transported Michigan on Canvas throughout the state in a specially designed 22-foot tractor trailer. Over 1.2 million Michiganians viewed the series at the state capitol, the state fair, art museums throughout the state, and of course at Hudson's. *Life* magazine even devoted four pages to highlight the collection. (Courtesy Michael Hauser.)

CIRCULATING LIBRARY, 1938. Hudson's circulating library was tucked away in a corner of the mezzanine. It was introduced in 1924 with one librarian and grew to six librarians at its peak in the 1940s. By that time, there were 30,000 registered patrons. (Courtesy Detroit Historical Museum.)

CELEBRATING HUDSON'S BIRTHDAY, 1941. This window, saluting Hudson's 60th anniversary, is devoted to the Pantry Shop located on the main floor. This popular department featured delicacies from around the world. Customers could even preorder everything from picnic lunches to Thanksgiving dinners from this unique shop. (Courtesy Detroit Historical Museum.)

PROMOTING PROPER USE OF THE DSR, 1945. Hudson's frequently devoted several of its windows to nonprofit organizations and public-service appeals. This window is educating members of the public about ways they could assist the DSR in providing efficient bus and streetcar service. (Courtesy Detroit Historical Museum.)

ANYONE FOR A PAS DE DEUX, 1947. Hudson's was a strong advocate for the arts and regularly profiled various art forms, such as this window promoting Ballet Russe de Monte Carlo. This dance company visited Detroit's Masonic Temple Theater annually from the 1940s through the 1960s, introducing the public to classical dance. (Courtesy Detroit Historical Museum.)

SALUTING ONE OF AMERICA'S OLDEST RADIO STATIONS, 1945. This Hudson's window celebrated the 25th anniversary of Detroit's WWJ radio. WWJ was one of America's first radio stations to broadcast regularly scheduled news reports, religious broadcasts, play-by-play sporting events, and original programs created by and sponsored by Hudson's. (Courtesy Detroit Historical Museum.)

A TRIBUTE TO KNUTE ROCKNE, 1931. Following his untimely death in a plane crash in 1931, Hudson's devoted a Woodward Avenue window to salute Knute Rockne. Rockne was head coach at the University of Notre Dame from 1918 to 1930. A street was named after him in Stevensville, Michigan, where he once maintained a summer home. (Courtesy Detroit Historical Museum.)

CELEBRATING DETROIT'S BIRTHDAY, 1951. Hudson's celebrated the 250th anniversary of the founding of Detroit with elaborate displays throughout the store. The company also published a special commemorative booklet, commissioned a series of paintings and dioramas, and sponsored festival parade floats. (Courtesy Detroit Historical Museum.)

FLAG DAY AT HUDSON'S, 1949. The unveiling of the world's largest flag on seven floors of Hudson's downtown store was a breathtaking sight that has been long remembered by thousands of Detroiters. More than a mile of rope was needed to hold the 1,600-pound flag to the building. (Courtesy Detroit Historical Museum.)

THE BOYS OF SUMMER, c. 1940. This Hudson's window promoted civic pride for the beloved Detroit Tigers. With the end of World War II and the return of Hank Greenberg and others from the military, the Tigers won the 1945 World Series. The photograph in the display was taken by renowned *Detroit News* photographer William Kuenzel. (Courtesy Detroit Historical Museum.)

HUDSONIAN

SALUTE TO OLD GLORY

THE FINAL UNFURLING OF OLD GLORY, 1976. A commemorative issue of *Hudsonian* captured the final public display of the grand flag in a series of images. Unsurpassed in size, the 25-year-old flag was presented to the Smithsonian Institution in 1976 as Hudson's contribution to the collection of items utilized to celebrate the 200th anniversary of the United States. (Courtesy Michael Hauser.)

Five

MEN'S AND WOMEN'S FASHIONS

HABERDASHERY AT ITS FINEST, 1941. This Hudson's window is promoting the introduction of colorful tones to Dobbs men's felt hat collection at the incredible price of $8.50 each. Dobbs, which was founded in the 1920s, was the premier manufacturer of men's dress hats. Until the early 1960s, men wore dress hats as a matter of course. (Courtesy Detroit Historical Museum.)

DARING TO BE COLORFUL, 1938. With the advent of socks being available in a multitude of colors, Hudson's devoted an entire window to men's hosiery. The display aided decision makers about what colors of socks worked well with suits and casual clothing. Part of this evolution was due to the introduction of nylon in the late 1930s. (Courtesy Detroit Historical Museum.)

FOR THE SPORTING GENT, 1937. The sports apparel department covered one half of the Grand River Avenue side of the second floor. Here guests could find attire for golfing, skiing, yachting, tennis, bowling, and hunting. Sports celebrities regularly visited Hudson's and often were guests on *Hudson's Sports Parade* on WJR radio. (Courtesy Detroit Historical Museum.)

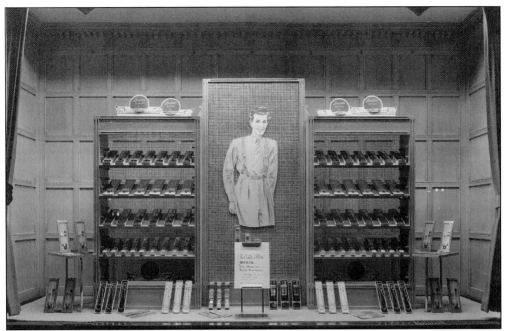

MEN'S ACCESSORIES WINDOW, 1941. This window displays the extensive line of Hickok men's accessories. Hickok was a prominent vendor at Hudson's from the 1940s through the 1970s, specializing in wallets, belts, key chains, suspenders, cuff links, and tie clasps. (Courtesy Detroit Historical Museum.)

THE FINE ART OF SHAVING, C. 1940. This whimsical Hudson's window is promoting the new Remington contour deluxe shaver. Remington introduced its first electric dry shaver, "the close shaver," in 1937. Early versions of electric razors were designed for dry skin only. Later versions allowed for shaving cream and moisture. (Courtesy Detroit Historical Museum.)

AAH . . . THE GOOD OLE SUMMERTIME, c. 1930. This Hudson's window is promoting the attributes of the Palm Beach brand of summer neckties. These ties were washable, easy to tie, smartly styled, and not susceptible to wrinkling. The signage refers to cravats, forerunners of the modern tailored necktie. (Courtesy Detroit Historical Museum.)

IF THE SUIT FITS, 1953. Men's suits, topcoats, and overcoats stretched for half a block on the second floor of the Woodward Avenue building. The custom tailoring center was located here, where men's clothing was made to a guest's exacting measurements. (Courtesy Detroit Historical Museum.)

PROMOTING ARROW SHIRTS AND COLLARS, 1950. This Hudson's window depicts the depth of style and selection the store offered for its best-selling white dress shirt. Guests also had a choice of collars, from pinpoint designs to spread collars. (Courtesy Detroit Historical Museum.)

PROMOTING ARROW SPORT SHIRTS, 1950. Most folks only knew Arrow for its line of dress shirts. During World War II, Arrow produced military uniforms. Following the war, the company expanded its line to include slacks, jackets, swimwear, and casual shirts. (Courtesy Detroit Historical Museum.)

Promoting Comfortable Fibers for Warm Weather, 1953. This Hudson's window focuses on rayon acetate men's suits. High tenacity rayon was first introduced in the 1940s, providing cool clothing comfort for warm summer months. (Courtesy Detroit Historical Museum.)

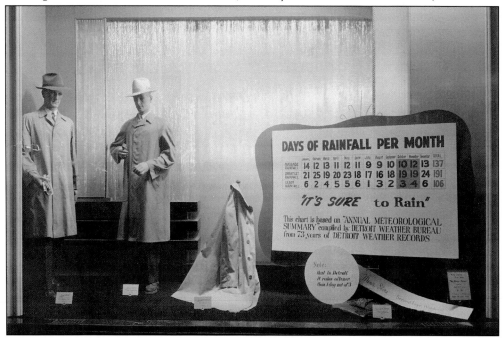

Charting the Weather to Promote Coats, 1947. With assistance from the Detroit Weather Bureau, this Hudson's window shows the importance of owning a raincoat. The chart depicts the average number of days it rains per month in Detroit, proclaiming, "In Detroit, it rains oftener than one day out of three." (Courtesy Detroit Historical Museum.)

THE FINAL WARDROBE TOUCH, 1954. Men's accessories were located on the Grand River Avenue end of the first floor of the Woodward Avenue building. Here guests could find ties, dress shirts, key chains, cuff links, pajamas, and robes. (Courtesy Detroit Historical Museum.)

PREPARING FOR COLLEGE, C. 1960. Through the years, the department for young men was known by various names such as The University Shop, College Corner, and the 1206 Shop. Here young men could be outfitted for suits, topcoats, sport coats, and other clothing items needed for a fashionable wardrobe. (Courtesy Detroit Historical Museum.)

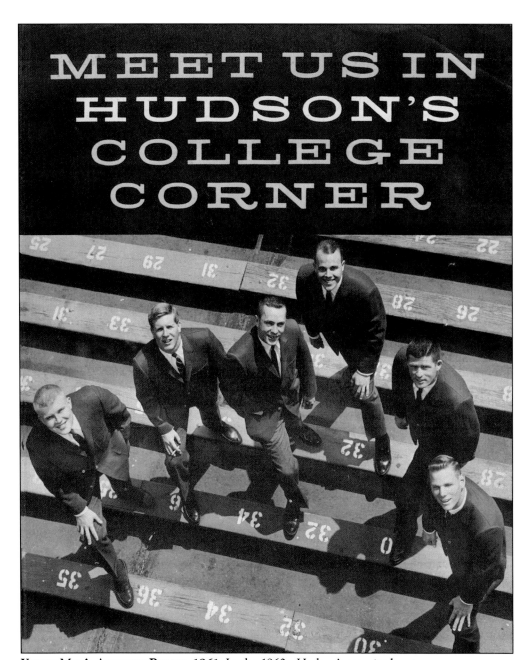

YOUNG MEN'S ADVISORY BOARD, 1961. In the 1960s, Hudson's recruited metro-area young men for its College Corner. This was an advisory board of six male college students well versed in styles and trends. Guests were encouraged to visit these in-store advisors regarding campus needs. (Courtesy Michael Hauser.)

McCall's Sewing Corps on the Road, 1941. An annual event was McCall's Magazine Sewing Corps in the Hudson auditorium. Guests could consult with McCall's and Hudson's stylists, who would advise on patterns, fabric, and color. Lucille Rivers, from *McCall's*, would present lectures and fashion shows previewing upcoming trends. (Courtesy Detroit Historical Museum.)

Anyone for a Warmer Climate? 1935. This cheerful department on the fifth floor was known as the South Shop and in later years as the Resort Shop. This area was very popular with Michiganders who traveled to Florida in the winter. Hudson's buyers shopped both the East and West Coast markets for swimwear and sporty attire. (Courtesy Detroit Historical Museum.)

WAITING TO BE PAMPERED, 1938. Hudson's Tourneur powder-blending salon was modernized in 1938 and moved to a new location on the fourth floor of the Farmer Street building. Tourneur specialists blended individual face powder for guests who patronized this shop. (Courtesy Detroit Historical Museum.)

SEVENTH-FLOOR MILLINERY SALON, 1942. As times and styles changed, the millinery salon at Hudson's followed suit and was completely renovated each decade. In this image, it has beautifully paneled walls and mirrors. The department was divided into multiple rooms, such as Debutante, Bridal, and Popular. (Courtesy Detroit Historical Museum.)

COMBINING SECURITY WITH STYLE, C. 1930. This Hudson's window depicts a new direction in handbags with the introduction of the fastened handbag by Talon. Mass production of zippers began in the 1920s with children's clothing and men's slacks. By the 1930s, zippers were acceptable in women's fashions. (Courtesy Detroit Historical Museum.)

THE SIXTH FLOOR OF LUXE, 1936. The leading fashion designers of the world were represented in Hudson's revamped moderne sixth floor. Here shoppers could find "high-grade dresses," misses and women's better dresses, moderately priced dresses, better coats, juniors and misses, and women's inexpensive dresses. (Courtesy Detroit Historical Museum.)

SIXTH-FLOOR DRESS AND COAT SALONS, 1936. This renovated area featured, according to *Hudsonian*, "Warm, medium brown French walnut paneling in French Empire classic proportions." These and other details, such as the wide expanse of space, provided a rich background for brilliantly colored apparel. (Courtesy Detroit Historical Museum.)

CHINESE HANDKERCHIEF PROMOTION, 1937. Imagine an entire department devoted to handkerchiefs. For this promotion, Hudson's sales associates dressed in Asian attire, and special displays were created for the exhibit cases. From embroidered versions to monogrammed styles, handkerchiefs for many years were a priority for holiday gift lists. (Courtesy Detroit Historical Museum.)

MAXIMUM WEAR WITH MINIMUM CARE, c. 1950. This Hudson's window is extolling the attributes of Everglaze evening dresses. Everglaze was a durable, starchless, and washable glaze finish. This fabric held its shape, resisted soiling and spotting, and was the ultimate in wrinkle resistance. (Courtesy Detroit Historical Museum.)

TOP-OF-THE-LINE LINGERIE, C. 1950. This Hudson's window is touting the Edith Lances line of bandeaux and long-line brassieres. Edith Lances, founded in 1930, produced the finest designer lingerie, swimwear, and sleepwear. Hudson's lingerie department was known for its attention to personal service. (Courtesy Detroit Historical Museum.)

FLAUNTING ONE'S FIGURE, 1950. This window is introducing an updated version of the Playtex Living Girdle, which was perforated all over and lined with cotton for ease of breathing. It was marketed along with the matching Playtex Living Bra. (Courtesy Detroit Historical Museum.)

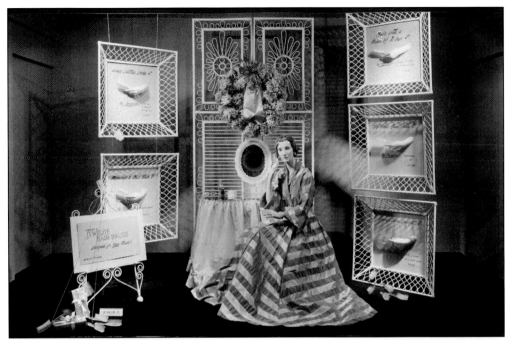

THE FINE ART OF BRUSHING, 1948. This Hudson's window is promoting Jewelite hairbrushes, aptly named "the aristocrat of plastics." Jewelite was a popular brand of brushes and combs made of acrylic and an early example of mass-consumer products. (Courtesy Detroit Historical Museum.)

HUDSON'S AND *VOGUE* MAGAZINE SALUTE TO PLYMOUTH, 1953. Automobiles regularly shared the spotlight with fashion at Hudson's. This promotion focused on the Belvedere, a conservative two-door hardtop introduced in 1951 and part of the Cranbrook series from Plymouth. (Courtesy Detroit Historical Museum.)

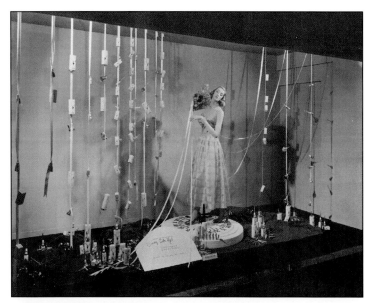

PROMOTING A NEW LINE FROM REVLON, 1950. Following World War II, consumer interest in apparel and fragrance gradually took hold again. As a result, Revlon introduced biannual nail enamel and lipstick promotions, which correlated with seasonal clothing introductions. (Courtesy Detroit Historical Museum.)

ENCHANTING FRAGRANCE WINDOW, 1947. At one time, Prince Matchabelli, known for its color-coded crown-shaped bottles, was one of the top five fragrance lines in Hudson's aisles of beauty. This window is promoting complimentary consultations with Del Russo, a makeup expert from the firm. (Courtesy Detroit Historical Museum.)

ACKNOWLEDGING WOMEN WHO WORK, 1952. This promotional tie-in between Hudson's and *Glamour* magazine was designed to woo the career woman, who prior to this time had been neglected. Both *Glamour* and *Charm* magazines were trailblazers in terms of positioning the working woman as an individual market segment. (Courtesy Detroit Historical Museum.)

SEVENTEEN MAGAZINE TIE-IN, 1945. *Seventeen* was the first national magazine to identify young women as a stable demographic to market to. Hudson's and its vendors joined forces to purchase national ads in *Seventeen* promoting the junior department. (Courtesy Detroit Historical Museum.)

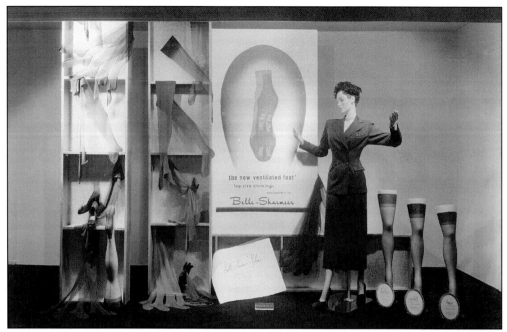

INTRODUCING VENTILATED NYLONS, 1948. Belle Sharmeer was a vaunted name in hosiery at Hudson's from 1938 to the 1960s. This line was sold individually to foot size, width, and length. Women liked Belle Sharmeer because of the better fit; the seams stayed straight, and there was a wide range of colors. (Courtesy Detroit Historical Museum.)

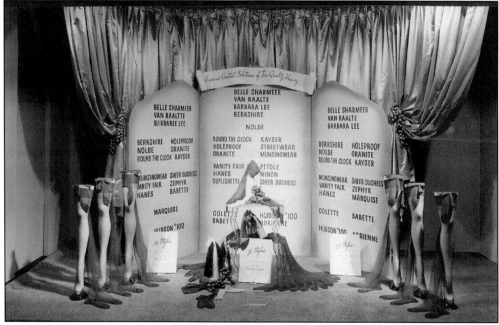

STOCKING SALUTE, 1948. Hudson's featured one of America's largest selections of women's hosiery. Typically the downtown store sold more than one million pairs of hose a year over the counter. The department boasted 25 brands and 567 different shades and tones. (Courtesy Detroit Historical Museum.)

READY TO HIT THE SLOPES, 1941. Detroit's largest department featuring women's winter sports togs was located on the fifth floor of Hudson's Woodward Avenue building. The winter sports shop regularly featured personal appearances by world-famous ski champions. (Courtesy Detroit Historical Museum.)

CHEERY, COLORFUL SUMMER FABRICS, 1948. This window is promoting Hudson's extensive selection of chambray fabrics for women who liked to sew. Chambray was smooth, strong, and closely woven, with a slight lustre. The fabric was easy to sew and laundered well. (Courtesy Detroit Historical Museum.)

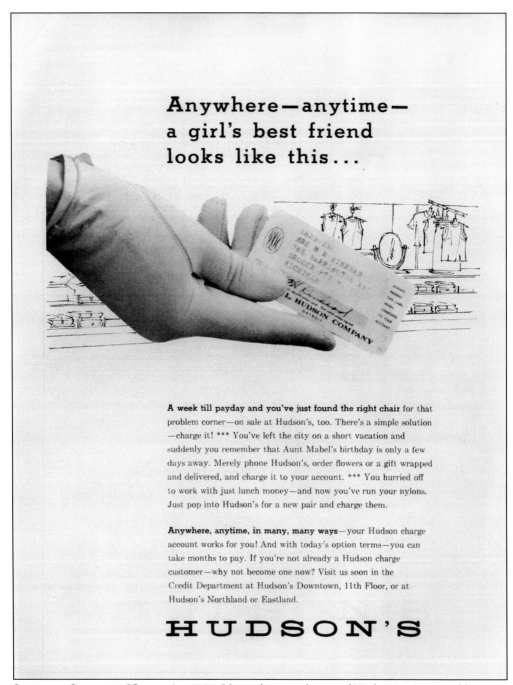

**Anywhere—anytime—
a girl's best friend
looks like this...**

A week till payday and you've just found the right chair for that
problem corner—on sale at Hudson's, too. There's a simple solution
—charge it! *** You've left the city on a short vacation and
suddenly you remember that Aunt Mabel's birthday is only a few
days away. Merely phone Hudson's, order flowers or a gift wrapped
and delivered, and charge it to your account. *** You hurried off
to work with just lunch money—and now you've run your nylons.
Just pop into Hudson's for a new pair and charge them.

Anywhere, anytime, in many, many ways—your Hudson charge
account works for you! And with today's option terms—you can
take months to pay. If you're not already a Hudson charge
customer—why not become one now? Visit us soon in the
Credit Department at Hudson's Downtown, 11th Floor, or at
Hudson's Northland or Eastland.

HUDSON'S

SECURING CREDIT AT HUDSON'S, 1964. Upon the completion of Hudson's 15-story addition in
1925, the store introduced its famous charge identification coin, the forerunner of today's charge
cards. A coin office was established on the mezzanine to assist guests. The purpose of the coin
was to greatly facilitate shopping by Hudson's charge customers. (Courtesy Michael Hauser.)

You ought to have
a Hudson Charge
...it's such a convenience

Whether you're shopping for one of Hudson's Great Home Sale values, selecting your new wardrobe or getting a quick manicure on your lunch hour—a Hudson Charge helps make it all so simple. With your Hudson credit plate in your pocket or handbag--you are ready to take advantage of sale prices as they appear, flattering new fashions as you see them and services as you need them. And, of course, with today's Option Terms you can spread your payments over many months. If you're not already a Hudson charge customer, we invite you to check the advantages now. Visit Hudson's Credit Department, Downtown, 11th; or ask at any Hudson store.

HUDSON'S

JUST SAY CHARGE IT, 1962. At one time, the only form of consumer credit available to working people was a Hudson's charge card. Store charge accounts made shoppers surprisingly loyal. Social hierarchy among department stores allowed shoppers to establish their own identities. The arrival of bank cards in the 1960s provided consumers credit nearly everywhere, ending loyalty to any one store. (Courtesy Michael Hauser.)

De Soto assembly line

Detroit tradition . . . building for the Future

a Hudson tradition . . .

building for your Fashion Future

Dior dramatizes the bell silhouette . . .

a Woodward Shop Salon

fashions it with beautifully simple bodice

adds box pleats all around the full, full skirt.

In gray silk and wool, punctuated with

black braid. From the Christian Dior-

New York collection . . . and found

in Hudson's Woodward Shops of course!

HUDSON'S

DETROIT

DEVELOPING PRESTIGE WITH DESIGNERS, 1950. Hudson's ran a series of image building ads in national magazines including *Town and Country* and *Vogue*. The ad shown here correlates Dior fashion tradition with the Dodge Chrysler assembly line. These ads generated not only goodwill but plenty of mail and phone orders as well. (Courtesy Michael Hauser.)

Sunlight, sun bright: our '66 Mirsa knit collection is set for the resort season in the LaSalle Room. Other bright ideas are yours for the basking in Hudson's Travel Shop—Both Downtown, 7th.

HUDSON'S
the Woodward Shops

HUDSON'S WOODWARD SHOPS, 1966. This collection of specialty shops, which stretched across the entire length of the seventh floor in the Woodward Avenue building, was promoted as Detroit's avenue of fashion. Renowned designers from around the globe had their collections represented here. The entire floor received a major makeover in 1962. (Courtesy Michael Hauser.)

PAMPERED FEET, 1953. Hudson's shoe salon for women was divided into four distinct sections. The leisure footwear shop specialized in slippers and play shoes. Other sections included street and dress shoes, sports and corrective shoes, and higher-priced styles for the well-heeled guest. (Courtesy Detroit Historical Museum.)

DRESSES FOR ALL AGES AND STYLES, 1965. In the mid-1960s, Hudson's completely renovated its various dress departments and categorized them by lifestyle. Dresses became the top-selling category in women's fashions in the 1920s, but by the 1960s casual sportswear was gradually becoming the everyday dress for women. (Courtesy Detroit Historical Museum.)

Six

THE HOME STORE

GRAND RAPIDS'S FINEST, 1953. Hudson's was one of a select group of U.S. department stores to feature an entire gallery of Baker Furniture, which was manufactured in Grand Rapids, Michigan. In 1953, Hudson's hosted a special exhibit of over 400 pieces of handcrafted furnishings from Baker. (Courtesy Detroit Historical Museum.)

HUDSON'S NINTH-FLOOR MODERN FURNITURE GALLERIES, C. 1950. Following World War II, furniture sales increased with the explosive development of Detroit's suburbs. Hudson's expanded the furniture department with a modern gallery stocked with California-style furnishings, modular designs, and streamlined styles in bold colors and fabrics. (Courtesy Detroit Historical Museum.)

HUDSON'S LEATHER FURNITURE GALLERY, 1953. In its heyday, Hudson's furniture floor housed 35 decorated model rooms on the ninth floor. In these various galleries, a guest could shop for styles from Baker, Dunbar, Heritage, Henredon, Knoll, Tomlinson, and The Pine Shops. (Courtesy Detroit Historical Museum.)

Holy Sepulcher Mausoleum furnished by Hudson's in a comfortable, dignified manner that offers an air of quiet serenity to the visitor.

Clubs, hotels, schools, hospitals
All kinds of institutional work

Hudson's Contract Department gives every
project expert personal attention!

Maybe you're opening a specialty shop, a club or a clinic . . . in any case
you can count on Hudson's Contract Department to give it the kind of interior you desire.
Our trained consultants offer excellent advice on color and style . . .
give estimates on draperies, floor coverings and furniture.
We've handled such varied projects as the First Presbyterian Church of Birmingham,
the Beaumont Hospital and the Verheyden Funeral Home. Why not give us a call today!

THE J. L. HUDSON COMPANY
Contract Department—11th Floor—Gratiot—D; Call CApitol 3-5100, Ext. 3286

HUDSON'S CONTRACT DIVISION, C. 1955. The Contract Division, initially located on the 11th floor, later moved to larger quarters on the 13th floor. This department sold furnishings, floor coverings, and window treatments to commercial and institutional clients. (Courtesy Michael Hauser.)

HUDSON'S STUDIO OF INTERIOR DESIGN, 1948. One of the most important divisions of home furnishings was the Design Studio. This service was dedicated to the idea of bringing beauty into a guest's home. It was a service whereby Hudson's advised any homemaker—of limited, moderate, or large means—on ways to achieve the most pleasing and artistic home décor. (Courtesy Detroit Historical Museum.)

FINE ARTS GALLERY, 1954. This gallery was established on Hudson's eighth floor in 1928 and originally encompassed four large exhibition rooms. Items displayed here ranged from inexpensive small color prints to large paintings created by old masters. Periodically the store showcased exhibits by local artists. (Courtesy Detroit Historical Museum.)

LET THERE BE LIGHT, C. 1950. Another enlarged department, warm in color and picturesque in setting on the 11th floor, was Lamps. Table lamps, bridge lamps, and floor lamps were offered with shades of every hue and kind and artistic bases of wood, metal, or clay. (Courtesy Detroit Historical Museum.)

IN-STORE DEMONSTRATION, C. 1960. This Hudson's associate is demonstrating to a guest in the eighth-floor drapery department the marvels of Scotchgard, a new way to protect upholstered fabric. 3M began selling the Scotchgard product in 1956 and finally received a patent for it in 1973. (Courtesy Detroit Historical Museum.)

TRIMZ WALLPAPER, 1948. Trimz was a popular wallpaper during the 1940s that was ready pasted, pretrimmed, and sold in single or double rolls. It was promoted as a fun way to enhance a room; all someone had to do was "cut it, dip it and up it goes." (Courtesy Detroit Historical Museum.)

BEFORE THERE WAS A PRINCE OF CHINTZ, C. 1950. Chintz was a cotton fabric usually glazed and printed with colorful floral designs. Hudson's eighth-floor Chintz Shop was a staple from the 1920s. Chintz was used primarily in the design of draperies and slipcovers. (Courtesy Detroit Historical Museum.)

LET'S HEAR SOME TUNES, C. 1940. Sparton Radios had a prominent presence in Hudson's 13th-floor music store. Sparton manufactured radios and phonographs in nearby Jackson, Michigan, from 1925 to 1956. The company also produced a line of televisions from 1948 to 1956. (Courtesy Detroit Historical Museum.)

MOHAWK RUG GALLERY, C. 1940. For many years, Mohawk, the largest carpet manufacturer in the United States, was the only vendor that produced all domestic weaves of carpeting. Hudson's eighth-floor gallery featured a venetian wall made up of multiple sections that could display dozens of styles and colors. (Courtesy Detroit Historical Museum.)

COLORIZING YOUR FLOORS, MID-CENTURY STYLE, 1949. In the late 1940s and 1950s, Hudson's sold acres and acres of colorful linoleum from Pabco Industries. Pabco's linoleum was soil-sealed and featured bold colors including turquoise, orange, and brown. Guests flocked to the eighth floor seeking new ideas for kitchens, baths, rec rooms, and basement floors. (Courtesy Detroit Historical Museum.)

HANDYMAN AT HUDSON'S, c. 1930. The Woodcraft Shop featured tools from Duro Metal Products, whose slogan was "tools of progress." This shop featured table saws, drill presses, band saws, routers, grinders, and belt sanders. Duro products were marketed to high-end home users, as depicted by the well-dressed businessmen seen here. (Courtesy Detroit Historical Museum.)

SPARKLING CRYSTAL, c. 1950. The resurgence of crystal in the late 1940s prompted Hudson's to display glassware in more sophisticated settings such as showcases and backlit niches. Guests were actually encouraged to touch the product, which resulted in soaring sales at the gift and bridal registries. (Courtesy Detroit Historical Museum.)

AMERICA'S GLASSMAKER, 1945. This Hudson's window was devoted to Toledo's Libbey Inc., the leading producer of popularly priced glass tableware in the United States. Up until World War II, Libbey had been producing a line of crystal known as Modern American. Following the war, Libbey scored a win with prepackaged sets of tumblers. (Courtesy Detroit Historical Museum.)

GLEAMING SILVER GALLERIES, 1948. The silver galleries on Hudson's tenth floor resembled a museum setting. Patrons could view sterling, silverplate, and stainless dinnerware in large showcases and cabinets. Chairs were plentiful to provide total comfort for guests. (Courtesy Detroit Historical Museum.)

DINNER IS SERVED, 1950. Hudson's housewares department regularly promoted Oneida's famous Community line of silver plate and sterling flatware. By 1960, research and development improved the quality of stainless steel, allowing Oneida the opportunity to successfully produce upgraded stainless steel patterns. (Courtesy Detroit Historical Museum.)

POPULAR DISHWARE ON DISPLAY, C. 1950. Hudson's 10th-floor china department included famous Blue Ridge Pottery, which was manufactured in Tennessee from the 1930s through the mid-1950s. This dinnerware was known for its underglaze decoration and bright, colorful patterns. These durable, hand-painted pieces are collector's items today. (Courtesy Detroit Historical Museum.)

IMPORTED CHINA, 1950. This Hudson's window is promoting the latest imported china from the Far East. Foreign imports, using less expensive production methods, provided tough competition for American producers. Postwar Japan became a major producer of dinnerware and pottery. (Courtesy Detroit Historical Museum.)

PROMOTING THE ATTRIBUTES OF ALUMINUM WARE, 1930. This Hudson's window is promoting the complete line of WearEver aluminum ware. This cookware had a strong appeal with homemakers because it was attractive, durable, and lightweight. Aluminum ware did not tarnish like silver and did not rust. (Courtesy Detroit Historical Museum.)

KITCHEN HELPERS, 1952. This Hudson's window is touting the newest way to dry dishes—with Rubbermaid dish drainers. Rubbermaid originally manufactured toy balloons but branched out to household products in 1934. The company today is known for its line of food storage, home organizers, and refuse container products. (Courtesy Detroit Historical Museum.)

HOOVER VACUUM DISPLAY, C. 1947. The major appliance department on Hudson's 10th floor was renovated in 1947 to emphasize style, convenience, and efficiency. Hudson's internal architects and merchandising offices worked for months to create handsome exhibits and a floor plan designed to funnel traffic into the department. (Courtesy Detroit Historical Museum.)

COMPETING WITH DISCOUNTERS, 1965. This Hudson's window, promoting Westinghouse appliances, was part of an aggressive policy against the growing popularity of discount stores. Hudson's comparison shoppers checked prices daily all over town to make sure the store's prices were consistently competitive. (Courtesy Detroit Historical Museum.)

EARLY REFRIGERATORS, 1935. Coolerators were cabinets that resembled old-fashioned pie safes. They were promoted as "air-conditioned" refrigerators, providing several shelves for perishable foods. Attributes of the coolerator were safe temperatures and balanced moisture. (Courtesy Detroit Historical Museum.)

KELVINATOR REFRIGERATOR SHOW, 1935. Hudson's began staging refrigerator shows on the 10th floor in 1929. These shows featured almost 100 models from the leading manufacturers, including Kelvinator, which was founded in Detroit in 1914. Kelvinator introduced the first automatic defrost model side-by-side refrigerator in the early 1950s. (Courtesy Detroit Historical Museum.)

TUBULAR CHROME FURNISHINGS, 1949. The late 1940s brought an onslaught of companies promoting chrome folding chairs and tables. Even Jane Russell got into the act as a spokesperson. Supposedly they were even strong enough to stand on. Selling points included long wearing usefulness, stain-resistant tops, and bright decorator colors. (Courtesy Detroit Historical Museum.)

CASUAL LIFESTYLES, 1948. This Hudson's window is touting the introduction of Samson Tables by Samsonite. The line included folding tables and chairs that were promoted as a "decorating scheme for budget homes" to be placed in a kitchen, nook, or den. (Courtesy Detroit Historical Museum.)

AND AWAY WE GO! 1933. Hudson's extensive luggage department specialized in luggage and trunks from the Wheary Trunk Company. Wheary manufactured steamer trunks, wardrobes, and aviator luggage. The department is decorated with beautifully framed travel posters. (Courtesy Detroit Historical Museum.)

TIME TO TEE OFF, 1920s. Hudson's golf department on the second floor provided a country club–like atmosphere for its collection of clubs, bags, balls, and related items. The store for a number of years even offered a golf school, enrolling pupils daily. (Courtesy Detroit Historical Museum.)

Leaving on a Jet Plane, 1953. Each year, Hudson's staged an international exhibition to highlight goods and services imported from other countries. At the event initially called Fair Internationale, various countries' flags were flown high above the marquee; throughout the store there were bazaars and ethnic restaurant specials. (Courtesy Detroit Historical Museum.)

For Those with a Green Thumb, c.1940. Hudson's garden center expanded from its 10th-floor home to the 12th-floor auditorium each spring. A special telephone order department was set up as well to handle calls generated from the 24-page garden book distributed at that time. Longtime vendors included Scott's and Ferry Seeds. (Courtesy Detroit Historical Museum.)

Custom Colorizing Revolution, 1947. The Martin Senour Company selected Hudson's to be one of the first in America to offer its Nu Hue paints. This "prescription mixing" color system offered 1,000 different paint tints, tones, and shades to match or harmonize with a guest's particular color selection. (Courtesy Detroit Historical Museum.)

ENJOY A RAINBOW OF SAVINGS IN

HUDSON'S

COLORFUL

WHITE

SALE

No need to search for the end of the rainbow—just hurry to Hudson's and find your own pot of gold. Sheets, cases, pillows, towels, table linens, everything you need—and all at savings a working girl appreciates. Shop now, stock up for months to come, watch your homemaking dollars stretch with ease as you select from beautiful pastels, vibrant jewel tones and snowy whites, as well. Find these values at Hudson's Downtown, Third; also available at Hudson's Northland, Fourth; and at Eastland, Third.

ANNUAL WHITE SALES, 1963. One of Hudson's most anticipated sales events for Michigan homemakers was the biannual white sale. This twice-yearly event took place in January and July to bolster business in typically slow sales months. By the 1960s, the sale took a more colorful role as manufacturers introduced bold colors and patterns. (Courtesy Michael Hauser.)

A LITTLE BIT OF EVERYTHING, 1950. The notions department at Hudson's initially was comprised of sewing items such as needles and thimbles. By the 1950s, the area also encompassed closet accessories, hair ornaments, sunglasses, and many impulse items that shoppers tend to find at dollar stores today. (Courtesy Detroit Historical Museum.)

TICKTOCK, 1953. The clock shop at Hudson's featured many different styles from a number of famous manufacturers. The selection included mantel clocks, schoolhouse clocks, regulators, office clocks, and alarm clocks. This display features French clocks as part of the Fair Internationale promotion. (Courtesy Detroit Historical Museum.)

Seven
DOWNTOWN WAREHOUSES

FIRST DISTRIBUTION CENTER, 1916. This facility was the first building conceived for Hudson's delivery functions and the company's first off-site location, located a half mile east of the downtown store on Beacon Street. In 1920, this structure was enlarged to 100,000 square feet. (Courtesy Detroit Historical Museum.)

BEACON STREET ENTRANCE, 1999. In 1924, Warehouse no. 2 was constructed, and by 1925 the Hudson's warehouse complex and distribution center encompassed 255,000 square feet. Primary functions at this facility, which employed 300 associates, were the distribution of merchandise, workrooms, and storage of reserve stocks. (Courtesy Michael Hauser.)

EXPANSE OF WAREHOUSE COMPLEX ON BEACON STREET, 1999. Hudson's mammoth warehouse complex housed nearly 100 loading docks, delivery bins, routing rooms, and parcel post rooms on the first floor. The second floor was devoted to workrooms for all home furnishings departments, while floors three through six were reserved for large and bulk merchandise storage. (Courtesy Michael Hauser.)

RECENT IMAGE OF ORIGINAL DISTRIBUTION CENTER, 1999. In the 1920s and 1930s, Hudson's had over 90 trucks in operation for delivery of packages, parcels, appliances, and furniture. The store's motor vehicles, operated by over 120 drivers, traveled 1.8 million miles a year and delivered 7.1 million parcels to 117 communities. (Courtesy Michael Hauser.)

CROSSOVER WITH MADISON CENTER IN BACKGROUND, 1999. In 1937, the Madison Avenue delivery building was constructed between Beaubien and Brush Streets. Containing 160,000 square feet, the first three floors were designed for speedy package distribution with a modern conveyor system. The fourth floor was reserved for workrooms. (Courtesy Michael Hauser.)

DOCKS AND CROSSOVERS, 1999. By 1945, Hudson's Warehouse no. 1 now consisted of 785,000 square feet, filling out the entire block bounded by Adams, Beaubien, Beacon, and Brush Streets. In a year's time, this warehouse would typically handle almost 400 truckloads of incoming merchandise, including almost 200,000 units of furniture. (Courtesy Michael Hauser.)

EXPANSE ALONG ADAMS STREET, 1999. Hudson's warehouse compound by 1950 spanned 22 acres and employed several hundred associates. A branch unit of the downtown store hospital also opened here in 1950. As a result of ever-rising parcel delivery costs, a campaign was instituted to encourage "take with" transactions at the downtown store. (Courtesy Michael Hauser.)

CLOSE-UP OF WAREHOUSE NO. 2, 1999. Hudson's famous warehouse sales had their beginnings in the downtown store prior to moving over to the warehouse compound. Thousands of bargain hunters will forever remember riding the enormous freight elevators, with the smells of fresh popcorn and frankfurters wafting through the air. (Courtesy Michael Hauser.)

CLOSE-UP OF WAREHOUSE NO. 1, 1999. In 1954, three additional floors were added to this part of the compound, now boasting 25 acres and occupying six floors. Floor men were added on each level to assist warehouse supervisors. This additional space was needed to house incoming merchandise for Hudson's new Northland store. (Courtesy Michael Hauser.)

You'll have to get up early to beat Mr. Shirley®!
(The ultimate Warehouse Sale shopper)

HUDSON'S WAREHOUSE SALE

Open Friday, Sept. 21 & Saturday, Sept. 22 at 8 a.m.
Shop Friday until 8 p.m., Saturday until 5 p.m.

MR. SHIRLEY AD, 1983. Hudson's introduced Mr. Shirley in the early 1980s as a marketing tool for the warehouse sales. He appeared in television, radio, and print media. This decade also saw the furniture area greatly expanded and the addition of display props, VCRs, cameras, and merchandise from the Rainbow Budget Store. (Courtesy Michael Hauser.)

two big sale days only:

Friday, January 5
Saturday, January 6

open both days at 8 a.m.
shop Friday to 8 p.m.; Saturday to 5 p.m.

20% to 60% off
original prices of everything in our $4,000,000 sale

- upholstered furniture
- bedroom furniture
- living room furniture
- dining room furniture
- entertainment centers
- tables • desks • wall units
- recliners
- Hide-A-Beds®
- mattresses

- small electrics
- pictures and frames
- VCRs
- stereos • TVs
- carpeting, area rugs
- pillows
- plants
- lamps
- furs

EXTRA 10% SAVINGS*

Did you see it at the last Warehouse Sale? If it's an electronics item, it's been reduced an additional 10% for this weekend's sale. And any piece of furniture or machine made area rug that was in our last sale has been reduced an additional 10%.
*Special Purchases Excluded

Hudson's Warehouse Sale

BAGGING SOME INCREDIBLE DISCOUNTS, 1983. Hudson's final downtown warehouse sale commenced on May 2, 1998. The company sold the entire warehouse compound to clear the way for Ford Field, the new home of the Detroit Lions pro football team. This property was the last vestige of Hudson's in the city of Detroit. (Courtesy Michael Hauser.)

INTERIOR OF DISTRIBUTION CENTER, C. 1960. Through the years, Hudson's operated warehouses and service centers all over town. Parade floats were assembled at Fort and Twelfth Streets, and large furniture fixtures were built at Clark Street and West Jefferson Avenue. Other facilities were at St. Antoine Street and East Grand Boulevard, on West Warren Avenue in Dearborn, High Street near Jefferson Avenue in Ecorse, and 230 East Grand River Avenue. (Courtesy Michael Hauser.)

Eight

BRANCHING OUT TO NORTHLAND

SOMETHING BIG IS ABOUT TO HAPPEN, 1952. Hudson's executives review plans for Northland with representatives from Victor Gruen Associates. They are, from left to right, Richard Webber, chairman of the board; Oscar Webber, president; James B. Webber, vice president and general manager; and Foster Winter, treasurer. (Courtesy Foster Winter.)

OFFICIAL GROUND-BREAKING FOR NORTHLAND, MAY 7, 1952. Initially Hudson's management was steadfastly against branching out to suburbia. However, witnessing the spectacular growth of suburban Detroit and ensuing competition, Oscar Webber decided that "we should get our portion of that business." Thus Northland, 12 miles from the downtown store, was born. (Courtesy Foster Winter.)

READY, SET, OPEN! 1954. Hudson's Northland officially opened on March 12, 1954. Five-year-old Jerry Webber (center) opened the store with the same key that was utilized to open the original Hudson store in 1881 on the main floor of the former Detroit Opera House on Campus Martius. (Courtesy Foster Winter.)

AERIAL VIEW OF NORTHLAND, 1954. Northland Center, the largest regional shopping center in the country upon opening in 1954, was another example of the vision and courage of Hudson's management. Built at a cost of $20 million, Northland was owned and operated as a subsidiary of Hudson's. It also became one of metro Detroit's top tourist attractions. (Courtesy Foster Winter.)

To All Hudsonians

This is to inform you, in advance of the public announcement tomorrow, of our plans for a second Regional Shopping Center, to be built in Detroit's Northwest Section. A large Hudson branch store will be the main unit in the new expansion project.

Development of this second Center depends upon approval ...Southfield Township authorities and the consent of the ...le who live in the area. Two large sites have been ...d, covering more area than the Eastland Center ...nt.

...land covers about 309 acres, bounded on the ...ile Road, on the north by Nine Mile Road, ...Greenfield Road. On the west, a large ...extends to Couzens (Northwestern) ...rea, containing nearly 100 acres, ...extends west to Southfield.

...he Shopping Center within ...Seward Mott, nationally ..., has been retained by ...e area. Cooperating ...ll recommend the ...nch.

...ure of the ...the land

SHOPPING DIRECTORY at HUDSON'S NORTHLAND

NOTICE TO ALL HUDSONIANS AND STORE DIRECTORY, 1954. Hudson's Northland was built on a grand scale, when retailers in the United States thought it was a smart idea to reproduce their downtown flagship stores as landmarks in the suburbs. The opening of Northland was extensively covered by national and international media, becoming an overnight success soon eclipsing the downtown store in sales. (Courtesy Michael Hauser.)

HUDSON'S CAR CARE CENTER, 1950S. Hudson's tire center was located on Greenfield Road at Northland Drive on the east side of the center. This facility was planned to satisfy the desire of suburbanites to travel by automobile. To attract female guests, the showroom was carpeted, featured plants and flowers, and was mere steps from the store. (Courtesy Detroit Historical Museum.)

NORTHWESTERN HIGHWAY ENTRANCE, 1955. Eight weeks after opening in 1954, Hudson's Northland hired another 500 associates to handle the crush of guests. Sales zoomed from $30 million that year to $65 million in 1959. Over one quarter of all men's shirts in metro Detroit were purchased from Hudson's Northland. (Courtesy Detroit Historical Museum.)

HOLIDAY DISPLAY AT HUDSON'S NORTHLAND, 1956. Elaborate interior and exterior displays became a tradition at Hudson's Northland. Following the closure of downtown in 1983, this store became Hudson's flagship. Management in the 1990s attempted to recapture downtown customs by bringing back Santa and adding animated walk-through exhibits. (Courtesy Detroit Historical Museum.)

FREESTANDING SPECIALTY SHOPS, 1969. In the 1960s, Hudson's added a freestanding pantry shop and a garden center at Northland to better serve guests. Gift and fresh fruit baskets were popular items in the pantry shop. By 1974, the store added valet parking for the convenience of guests. (Courtesy Detroit Historical Museum.)

FOOT SUPPORT, 1954. The women's shoe salon at Hudson's Northland was an open area on the first level that featured mass displays and extra stock capacity. The island units proved to be perfect silent sales associates for self-selection. (Courtesy Michael Hauser.)

NORTHLAND DINING ROOM, 1954. Hudson's Northland Room on the fourth floor spanned 10,000 square feet and could seat 325 guests. This modern dining room offered full waitress service with a staff of 50 and served 1,200 lunches daily. Guests could enjoy time-honored downtown Hudson's favorites, including Maurice salad. (Courtesy Michael Hauser.)

LUNCHTIME FAVORITES, 1975. The Northland Room featured luncheon fashion shows each Monday during the 1950s and 1960s, filling the room with suburban women. As additional Hudson's stores opened, business at Northland declined, and the dining room closed in 1997. An expanded Marketplace Foods opened on the lower level for in-store dining and take-out. (Courtesy Michael Hauser.)

DRAMATIC MILLINERY DEPARTMENT, 1954. The millinery area at Northland exemplified the modern simplicity yet dramatic character of many of the store's departments. High ceilings, natural light from large plate-glass windows, and customized fitting stations all enhanced the guest service experience. (Courtesy Michael Hauser.)

JUNIOR BOYS AT NORTHLAND, 1954. This department was uncluttered and featured versatile open-selling units, making it simpler for guests to select items. Easy-to-read overhead signage also made for easier shopping for those with specific merchandise needs in mind. (Courtesy Michael Hauser.)

REACHING HUDSON'S NORTHLAND VIA MASS TRANSIT, 1954. This view shows the various ways guests could reach Hudson's Northland—easy vehicle access on the lower level and by bus on the upper level. More than 1 in 10 guests arrived by DSR coaches or Great Lakes Transit coaches via the 13 bus lines serving the center. (Courtesy Michael Hauser.)

POSTCARD VIEW OF NORTHLAND'S COURTYARD, 1954. The shopping experience at Hudson's Northland was enhanced by soothing gardens, fountains, and a wealth of outstanding sculpture. Northland proved to be a training ground for many top Hudson's executives as well as preparation training for branch stores. (Courtesy Michael Hauser.)

When, some thirty-odd years ago, we were looking for a suburban site for a
brand new store, Southfield was our first choice. We saw the potential for growth.
A happy blend of the urban and suburban, of residential and business areas.
A dynamic climate for Hudson's. So we built Hudson's Northland in Southfield.
Now our largest store. 550,000 square feet, newly rebuilt, redecorated and
restocked. Bustling with fashions for family and home, with the necessities and
rewards of life. Busy, successful and happy. Southfield, Hudson's thanks you!

hudson's

HUDSON'S SALUTES SOUTHFIELD ON ITS BIRTHDAY, 1983. On its 25th birthday, Hudson's ran
this ad commemorating the city of Southfield, where Northland is located. Hudson's completed a
major renovation of the Northland store in 1985, and Region One offices moved here in 1986 from
downtown. The furniture department doubled in size in 1987, taking over the former Rainbow
Budget Store space. (Courtesy Michael Hauser.)

Discover Thousands of Local History Books
Featuring Millions of Vintage Images

Arcadia Publishing, the leading local history publisher in the United States, is committed to making history accessible and meaningful through publishing books that celebrate and preserve the heritage of America's people and places.

Find more books like this at
www.arcadiapublishing.com

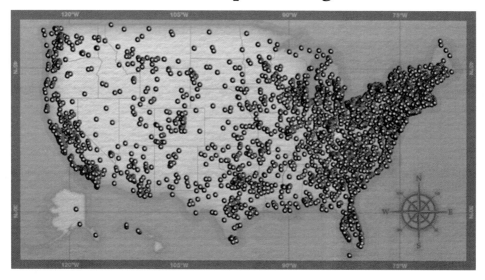

Search for your hometown history, your old stomping grounds, and even your favorite sports team.